The Birth of the American Navy

Jeremy Thornton

The Rosen Publishing Group's
PowerKids Press™
New York

For my wife, Tracee Sioux

Published in 2003 by The Rosen Publishing Group, Inc.
29 East 21st Street, New York, NY 10010

First Edition

Editor: Joanne Randolph
Designers: Michael J. Caroleo, Mike Donnellan, Michael de Guzman, Colin Dizengoff
Layout: Nick Sciacca

Photo Credit: Cover © North Wind Pictures; cover (portrait), p. 11 © Stock Montage/Superstock; back cover Library of Congress, Prints and Photographs Division; p. 4 © Francis G. Mayer/CORBIS; p. 7 © courtesy Winterthur Museum; p. 8 courtesy of the New-York Historical Society; p. 11 (inset) photo by Tom Cocchiaro, courtesy of The Ranger Foundation; p. 12 © Superstock; p. 15 © CORBIS; p. 16 (top) © Hulton/Archive/Getty Images; pp. 16 (bottom), 19 (inset), 20 (inset) Center for Legislative Archives, National Archives and Records Administration; p. 19 Still Picture Branch, National Archives and Records Administration; p. 20 © Giraudon/Art Resource, NY.

Thornton, Jeremy.
The birth of the American Navy / by Jeremy Thornton.
    p. cm. — (Building America's democracy)
Includes bibliographical references and index.
Summary: Briefly describes the early years of the United States Navy, during the Revolutionary War and just after, and touches on the activities of the Navy today.
ISBN 0-8239-6274-1 (library binding)
1. United States. Continental Navy—History—Juvenile literature. 2. United States. Navy—History—18th century—Juvenile literature. 3. United States. Navy—History—19th century—Juvenile literature. 4. United States—History, Naval—18th century—Juvenile literature. 5. United States—History, Naval—19th century—Juvenile literature. [1. United States. Continental Navy. 2. United States Navy—History—18th century. 3. United States—History, Naval—To 1900.] I. Title.
 VA56 .T48 2003
  359'.00973'09033—dc21
                                        2001006664

Manufactured in the United States of America

Contents

The American Revolution

During the American Revolution (1775–1783), the British had the most powerful navy in the world. They used their ships to control the east coast of North America. They attacked American cities, carried supplies and **reinforcements** to their troops, and captured American ships. The American congress **debated** whether or not Americans should form a navy to protect themselves. Some members of Congress thought the only way to fight the British navy was for America to form its own sea-fighting force. Others thought it would be impossible to create a navy strong enough to fight against British warships. At first each colony had to use its own ships, such as fishing or **merchant** ships, to try to protect itself.

The Battle of Bunker Hill, shown in this 1786 painting by John Trumbull, was one of the first major battles in the American Revolution. It was fought on June 17, 1775.

The Birth of the Continental Navy

In August 1775, George Washington began to charter, or rent, fishing boats and merchant ships to attack British ships. The fishing boat *Hannah* was the first ship that Washington sent to capture much-needed supplies from British ships that were on their way to Boston, Massachusetts. Meanwhile Congress decided to form a small navy. On October 13, 1775, Congress sent two ships to attack British supply ships. They established a **committee** of three members of Congress to lead the new navy. They appointed Esek Hopkins, a sea captain from Rhode Island, as commander in chief of the navy on December 22, 1775.

John Trumbull painted George Washington in his military uniform in this 1790 portrait. This is how Washington would have looked while commanding the Continental army.

THE *Privateer Ship*

Duke of Cumberland,

Capt. JAMES LILLY,

Mounting 16 SIX-POUNDERS, and is to carry 120 Men : Is now lying at the Watering-Place, and will proceed on her intended Cruize in a Week from the Date hereof : She is a compleat Ship and a prime sailer. All Gentlemen Seamen and others, who intend making a Cruize, are defired to repair on board.

Privateers

The American navy was not strong enough to fight the large British warships. Instead it attacked smaller British ships carrying supplies. On November 25, 1775, Congress also voted to allow **privateers** to attack the British vessels. Privateers were citizens who owned their own fishing and merchant ships. Much like pirates, these privateers would attack British ships and would steal valuables and supplies. Unlike pirates, the privateers acted legally. As payment for their help, the privateers were allowed to split the profits with the colonies. These ships were not part of the American navy, but they did help the navy fight the war.

In most early wars in America, there were not enough ships to act as a navy. Ads, such as this one, looking for privateers to protect the coast were placed in newspapers.

John Paul Jones

John Paul Jones was the most successful American ship captain of his time. He began his service in the navy on Esek Hopkins's **flagship**, the *Alfred*. Soon he was given command of his own ship, the *Ranger*. He sailed to Europe in 1777. Using **ports** in France as a base, he captured British ships and attacked British cities on the coast. On April 24, 1778, he captured the HMS *Drake* off the coast of Ireland.

Jones was very important to the American war effort, because he brought the war to Britain's shores. This scared the British and forced them to use part of their navy to defend their merchant ships and their coastline. This meant there were fewer British ships to fight across the ocean on the American coast.

John Paul Jones decided to help the patriot cause because he believed Americans had the right to be free from Britain. *Inset:* This is an accurate model of the *Ranger*.

"I have not yet begun to fight!"

John Paul Jones's most famous sea battle occurred on September 23, 1779. He was in command of the *Bonhomme Richard*. He met the British ship HMS *Serapis* off the coast of Yorkshire, Britain. The *Bonhomme Richard* was quickly hit by several full **cannon** shots along its side and lost the use of many of its guns. Jones needed to think quickly. He brought his ship close enough to the *Serapis* to tie the two ships together. After more firing, the *Richard* was in bad shape. The British captain, Richard Pearson, asked Jones if he would **surrender**. Jones yelled, "I have not yet begun to fight!" After almost four hours of terrible fighting, the *Serapis* surrendered. It was a great victory for the Americans.

The *Bonhomme Richard* was wrecked in this battle. Even though Jones and his men had won, they had to board the *Serapis* and let the *Richard* sink.

The French Help America

Over the course of the American Revolution, American ships captured close to 600 British ships. However, they suffered many defeats. The only naval victory for the Americans against an entire British **fleet** was actually won by the French, who had sided with the Americans against Britain. On September 5, 1781, George Washington's army fought British general Charles Cornwallis at Yorktown, Virginia. The French fleet, led by Admiral François-Joseph-Paul de Grasse, prevented the British fleet from arriving with reinforcements. This led to Cornwallis's surrender and to the end of the war. The peace agreement between America and Britain, the **Treaty of Paris**, was signed in 1783.

The French fleet, led by Admiral de Grasse, blocked the British from entering the harbor to bring supplies and more men to help Cornwallis.

Left: This is a portion of the Act passed by Congress allowing Washington to purchase six ships to form a navy.

The Barbary Pirates

When the war ended, Congress decided it could not afford to keep a navy. The colonies sold their ships. By 1785, the last ship of the American navy, the *Alliance*, had been sold. However, the Americans soon found that they couldn't protect their merchant ships. Pirates from the **Barbary States** in Africa were capturing American ships and were making slaves of their crews. Congress debated whether they should pay the Barbary States or other countries for protection or develop a permanent navy to protect American ships. Finally, in March 1794, Congress passed a law allowing President George Washington to buy six ships for a navy.

The Barbary pirates were badly interrupting U.S. trade with West Africa, a key stop on trading routes. In response the United States decided to bomb Tripoli.

The Department of the Navy

The first three ships of the new American navy, the USS *United States*, the USS *Constellation*, and the USS *Constitution*, were completed in 1797. By this time, there was a more pressing threat. The Napoleonic Wars had begun between France and Britain. The French were capturing all ships that traded with Britain, including American ships. On April 30, 1798, the Department of the Navy was officially established. In 1803, the focus returned to stopping the Barbary pirates of northern Africa. After the United States bombed the Barbary States and blocked their ports, the Barbary States agreed to leave U.S. ships alone. A treaty was signed between the United States, Tripoli, Tunisia, and Algiers.

The USS *Constitution* was one of six ships built for the U.S. Navy for use against the Barbary pirates. The ship was made from 7-inch-thick (17-cm-thick) oak planks.

A Bill

To establish an Executive department, to
be denominated the department of the
Navy.

1 SECTION 1. **BE** it enacted by the Senate and House of Repre-
2 sentatives of the United States of America, in Congress assembled,
3 That there shall be an Executive Department under the deno-
4 mination of the Department of the Navy, the chief officer of
5 which shall be called the Secretary of the Navy, whose duty it
6 shall be to execute such orders as he shall receive from the
7 President of the United States, relative to the procurement of
8 naval stores and materials and the construction, armament,
9 equipment and employment of vessels of war, as well as all
10 other matters connected with the Naval establishment of the
11 United States.

1 SECT. 2. And be it further enacted, That a principal clerk and
2 other clerks which he shall deem necessary, shall be ap-
3 pointed by the Secretary of the Navy, who shall be employed
4 in such manner as he shall deem most expedient. In case of the
5 vacancy of the chief clerk by removal or otherwise, it shall
6 be the duty of the principal clerk to take the charge and cus-
7 tody of all the books, records and documents of the said office.

1 SECT. 3. And be it further enacted, That the Secretary of the
2 Navy shall be authorised and he is hereby authorised and
3 empowered, immediately after his appointment and shall enter
4 upon the duties of his office, to take possession of all the re-
5 cords, books and documents, and all other matters and things
6 appertaining to this department, which are now deposited in
7 the office of the Secretary at war.

Bill to Establish the
Department of the Navy

Gentlemen of the Senate

I nominate Benjamin Stoddert of Maryland to be Secretary of the Navy, in the Place of George Cabott who has declined his appointment.

George Woodruff of Georgia to be Attorney for the District of Georgia in the Place of Charles Jackson resigned

Frederick William Lutze of Stetin in Prussia to be Consul of the United States at Stetin.

John Adams

United States May 1st
1798

Benjamin Stoddert

Benjamin Stoddert, a merchant from Maryland who had served as secretary for the Board of War, was made the first secretary of the navy in June 1798. He worked hard to strengthen the American navy. Stoddert used Britain's war with France, which lasted until 1801, as a reason to build more ships and to expand the U.S. Navy's activity. The French were attacking any ships, including American merchant ships, that traded with Britain. Stoddert used the new ships to protect Americans from being captured by the French. During this war, Captain Thomas Truxton of the USS *Constellation* captured two powerful French warships.

John Adams nominated Benjamin Stoddert for secretary of the navy on May 18, 1798. His nomination *(inset)* was accepted, and Stoddert took office in June.

The Navy Today

After the United States and France came to an agreement in 1801, many people thought there would no longer be a need for the U.S. Navy. However, the American navy was still necessary to protect merchant ships that were going to Europe and to Africa and later to fight Britain in the War of 1812. People finally realized that the U.S. Navy was an important part of the U.S. military, and the Navy continued to grow. Today the Navy guards the American coast. It protects friendly ships on the open seas, and it helps the rest of the U.S. military in protecting freedom around the world.

Glossary

Barbary States (BAR-buh-ree STAYTS) Countries located in northern Africa.

cannon (KA-nun) A large gun with a smooth bore barrel.

committee (kuh-MIH-tee) A group of people directed to oversee or to consider a matter.

debated (dih-BAYT-ed) To have argued or discussed.

flagship (FLAG-ship) A ship that carries the commander of the fleet and that flies his flag.

fleet (FLEET) Many ships under the command of one person.

merchant (MER-chint) One who buys, sells, or trades.

ports (PORTS) A city or town where ships come to dock and trade.

privateers (pry-vuh-TEERZ) Armed pirates licensed by the government.

reinforcements (ree-in-FORS-ments) Additional troops that strengthen an army.

surrender (suh-REN-dur) To give up.

Treaty of Paris (TREE-tee UV PAR-es) The name of an important peace agreement that ended the American Revolution, signed in Paris, France.

Index

Primary Sources

Page 4. *The Death of General Warren at the Battle of Bunker's Hill, June 17, 1775.* This oil painting, done in 1786 by John Trumbull, is held at the Yale University Art Gallery. **Page 7.** *Washington at Verplanck's Point.* John Trumbull painted George Washington in his military uniform in this 1790 portrait. The oil painting is held at the Winterthur Museum. **Page 8.** Privateer advertisement from the *New York Mercury,* December 4, 1758, during the Seven Years' War. This advertisement is from the collection at the New-York Historical Society. **Page 11.** This is an accurate model from the Ranger Society of the *Ranger,* including the modifications Jones made to improve its sailing ability. The Ranger Society will also create a full-size replica. **Page 12.** *Bonhomme Richard Vs the Serapis, September 23, 1779.* This painting by Thomas Butterworth, (1768–1852) a well-known artist of historic marine scenes, is not a completely accurate portrayal of the event, but does convey the drama of the battle. Also Jones's flag was the famous and unique flag now called the Serapis flag, but here the Stars and Stripes is flying. **Page 15.** *Reddition de l'Armée Angloises Commandée par Mylord Comte de Cornwallis aux Armées Combinées des États unis de l'Amérique et de France.* . . . This 1781 hand-colored etching is a fanciful French representation of the surrender at Yorktown, Virginia, depicted in the upper center as a walled medieval town. The French army, dressed in blue, is in the foreground and the American army, in red, is in the background, between which the British army is seen leaving the field. The French fleet is anchored in the York River. **Page 16.** *Act to Provide a Naval Armament.* This document is held by the National Archives and Records Administration in Washington, D.C. **Page 19.** *Bill to Establish the Department of the Navy.* This is a page from the bill passed by Congress on April 11, 1798. The drawing of the USS *Constitution* is a view from the starboard bow. Both items are held at the National Archives. The image on the right is a view from the starboard bow. **Page 20.** John Adams's letter to the Senate nominating Benjamin Stoddert to be Secretary of the Navy. This letter is held at the National Archives. The painting of John Adams is by George Peter Alesander Healy.

Web Sites

Due to the changing nature of Internet links, PowerKids Press has developed an online list of Web sites related to the subject of this book. This site is updated regularly. Please use this link to access the list:
www.powerkidslinks.com/bad/bamnavy/